Let's go UNDERGROUND!
Let's travel into the murky, muddy earth.
It's dark and damp down here.

There's no sunshine, no birdsong and no wind.
But it's a world BURSTING with life.

Do you want to find out more?

To Olive – B.L.

To Mi and Huy – X.L.

First published 2025 by Nosy Crow Ltd
Wheat Wharf, 27a Shad Thames,
London, SE1 2XZ, UK

Nosy Crow Eireann Ltd
44 Orchard Grove, Kenmare,
Co Kerry, V93 FY22, Ireland

www.nosycrow.com

ISBN 978 1 80513 069 7 (HB)
ISBN 978 1 80513 070 3 (PB)

'The National Trust' and the oak leaf logo are registered trademarks of The National Trust (Enterprises) Limited (a subsidiary of The National Trust for Places of Historic Interest or Natural Beauty, Registered Charity Number 205846).

Nosy Crow and associated logos are trademarks
and/or registered trademarks of Nosy Crow Ltd.

Text © Ben Lerwill, 2025
Illustrations © Xuan Le, 2025

The right of Ben Lerwill to be identified as the author and Xuan Le
to be identified as the illustrator of this work has been asserted.

All rights reserved.

This book is sold subject to the condition that it shall not,
By way of trade or otherwise, be lent, hired out or otherwise circulated in
any form of binding or cover other than that in which it is published.
No part of this publication may be reproduced, stored in a retrieval system,
or transmitted in any form or by any means
(electronic, mechanical, photocopying, recording or otherwise)
without the prior written permission of Nosy Crow Ltd.

The publisher and copyright holders prohibit the use of
either text or illustrations to develop any generative machine learning
artificial intelligence (AI) models or related technologies.

A CIP catalogue record for this book is available from the British Library.

Printed in China following rigorous ethical sourcing standards

1 3 5 7 9 8 6 4 2 (HB)
1 3 5 7 9 8 6 4 2 (PB)

WONDER WORLD
EARTH

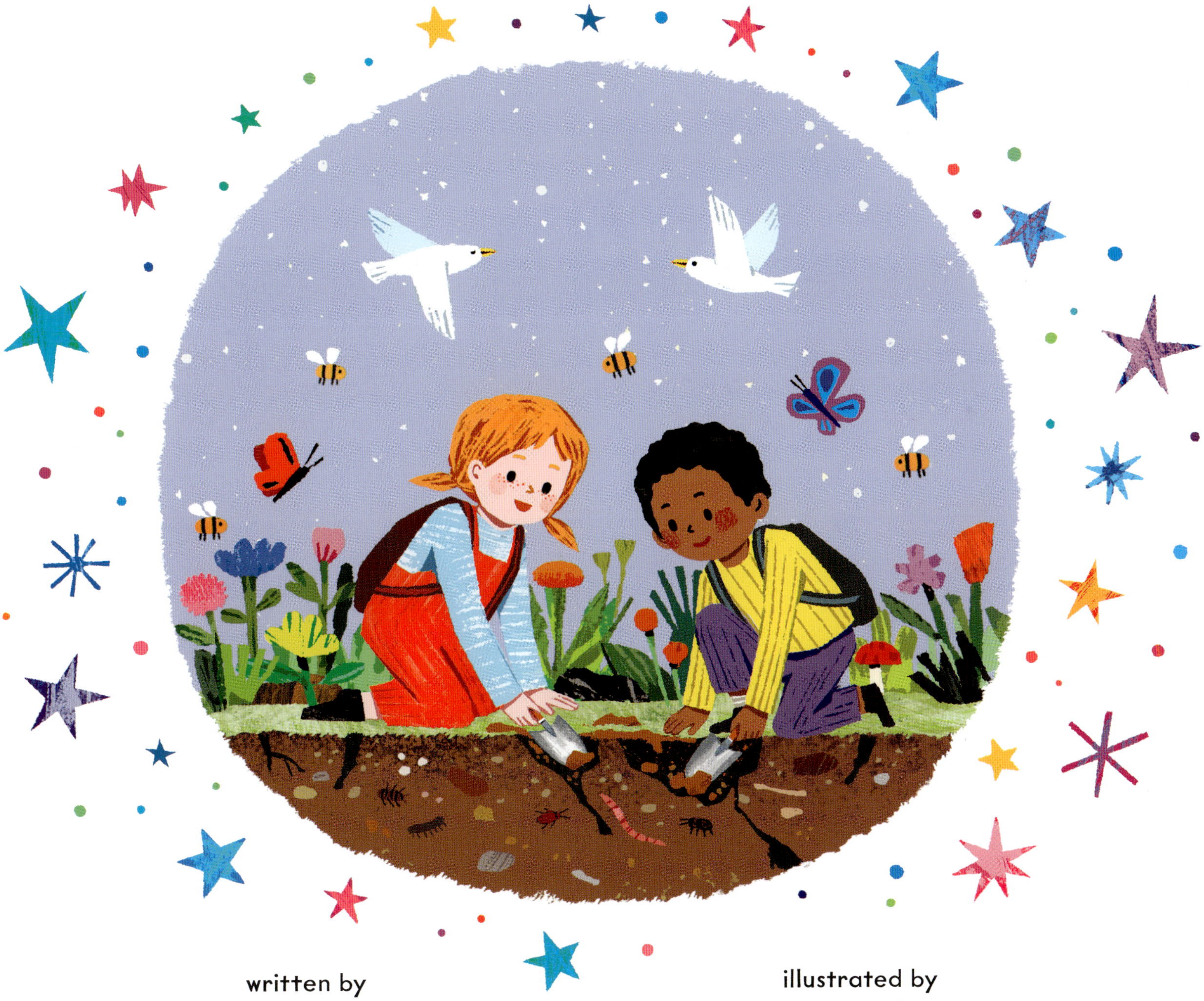

written by
Ben Lerwill

illustrated by
Xuan Le

This is the EARTH.

It's made up of different LAYERS of rock and metal.

At the very centre of our planet is a giant, solid, iron ball. It's nearly as hot as the surface of the Sun. We call it the INNER CORE.

INNER CORE

OUTER CORE

The next layer is called the OUTER CORE. It's as hot as the inner core, but it's runny rather than solid. It's a fiery swirl of two liquid metals: iron and nickel.

The thickest layer is called the MANTLE. It's made of very strong, **dense rock**. It's so **heavy** that it makes up more than 60 per cent of the Earth's weight.

MANTLE

The TOP layer is called the CRUST. It's **thinner** than the other layers. Like the mantle, it's made of different kinds of **rock**.

CRUST

The CRUST is also home to the most wonderful layer of all . . .

Different parts of the world have different kinds of soil.

Soil can be **thick** and **boggy**.

It can be **dry** and **powdery**.

It can be **heavy** and **chalky**.

It can even be **tough** and **frosty**.

Temperature, rainfall and different minerals all change how soil looks and feels. But wherever you go, soil contains...

...LOTS of LIFE!

This is an EARTHWORM. It's about the size of your little finger. It has no eyes, ears or nose, but it's a real underground HERO.

When it burrows through the soil, it helps air and water to spread underground.

It also eats lots of organic matter. When it poos it out, it makes the soil healthy.

Worms help to keep the soil FULL of nutrients, or energy, for our plants and trees.

There are many different kinds of worm...

Some WORMS are as LONG as a car.

Some could FIT onto a freckle.

Around the world there are
400 BILLION BILLION
worms in the soil!

Worms might be *slippery* and *squiggly*, but they're also one of the most **important** animals on the planet. As well as helping the soil, they're a VITAL part of...

... the world's FOOD CHAIN.

BIRDS such as jays, thrushes, robins, blackbirds and starlings pull UP worms from the ground and gobble them up.

MAMMALS such as bears, hedgehogs, weasels, foxes and warthogs dig DOWN into the soil to find them.

CREATURES such as beetles, centipedes, turtles, frogs and snakes all eat worms, too.

So, WORMS give the **soil** more **nutrients**...

the **soil** gives WORMS a home...

and WORMS give **animals a meal!**

Many other CREEPY-CRAWLIES live underground, too.
If you pick up a clump of soil and look closely,
you'll probably spot LOTS of
MINIBEASTS.

Maybe millipedes,

or grubs,

or slimy
slugs.

Maybe
earwigs,

or
termites,

or busy
ants.

In the same handful there are also THOUSANDS and
THOUSANDS of other creepy-crawlies...

Some help things grow by recycling nutrients for our plants and crops. Some act as food for TINY creepy-crawlies. Some even make OXYGEN for us to BREATHE.

Microbes are AMAZING!

And what ELSE lives UNDERGROUND?

About a **third** of all the **animals** in the world **live** UNDERGROUND – and NOT all of them are TINY...

MOLES tunnel through the soil looking for worms to eat.

RABBITS make underground **dens** to stay **warm** and **safe**.

PLATYPUSES sleep in burrows near the water's edge.

CHIPMUNKS spend the cold winter underground, nesting and eating.

Lots more animals live in the soil. Can YOU think of any?

When you walk through a FOREST...

the sky is full of trunks, branches and leaves.
But things are even busier in the soil!

Underground, the ROOTS of all the trees and plants spread out like a GIANT web.

Weaving among them are long, stringy strands of FUNGI, connecting everything together...

Some experts think the FUNGI in the soil might help keep the trees and plants **alive** by feeding them **water** and **nutrients** through their ROOTS.

They also think trees may **share** nutrients with each other through the FUNGI — and could even use the FUNGI as a **message network**, to WARN other trees about DANGERS such as **disease**.

The whole thing is like an ENORMOUS underground city where everything works together: the trees, the roots, the fungi, the microbes, the creepy-crawlies and the nutrients in the soil!

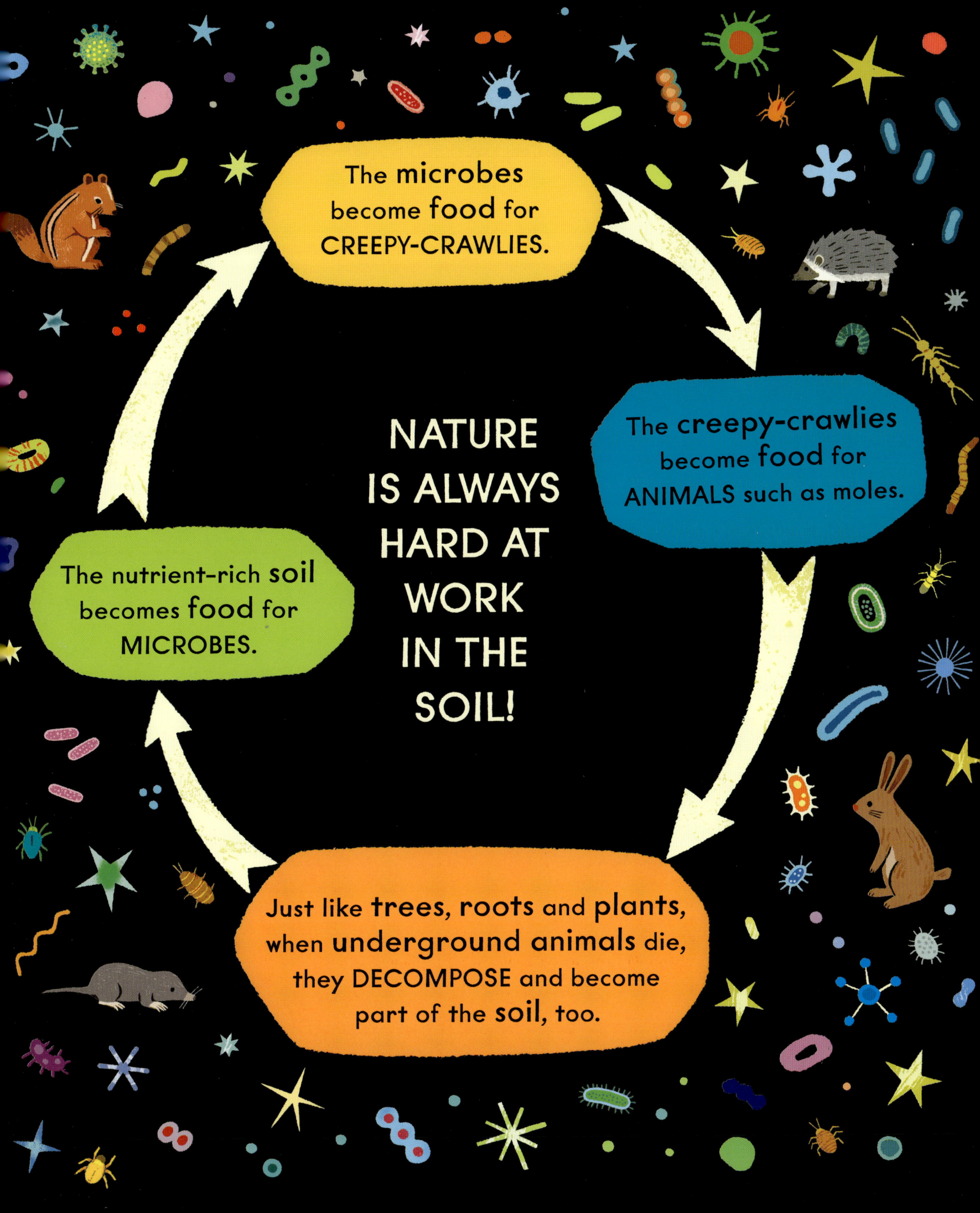

SOIL gives us OUR food too...

FRUIT TREES and VEGETABLES all need to grow in soil.
Without soil, there would be NO apples, tomatoes,
strawberries, bananas or cucumbers – or
any other fruits and vegetables!

FARM CROPS need to grow in soil, too. Without soil, there would
be NO bread, pasta, popcorn, chips, rice, chocolate or sugar.

And because FARM ANIMALS have to eat things grown in soil, there would be NO farm animals either...

So there would be NO eggs, butter, cheese, milk or meat.

Soil gives us LIFE!

SOIL has other VITAL jobs . . .

Soil absorbs CARBON DIOXIDE and keeps it safe.
Carbon dioxide is a **gas.** When we have **too much** of it in the **air,**
it makes the PLANET **warmer** than it should be.

By **storing** carbon dioxide **underground,**
healthy soil **helps** the world to stay at
the **right** TEMPERATURE.

Soil helps us to create **buildings**. By digging **down** before we build **up**, our houses, schools and hospitals can stand STRONG.

Soil soaks up rain. Tree and plant ROOTS in the soil help **stop** water from FLOODING across the land.

Soil **cleans** the water too, by helping **absorb** chemicals and bacteria.

All this is happening right **under** our **feet!**

SOIL is INCREDIBLE!

It's working day and night, ALL around the WORLD.

It's alive with TRILLIONS of living things, all helping to make our planet cleaner and greener.

Without soil, the world simply wouldn't be THE WORLD.

So the next time you pick up a handful of soil, remember that you're holding...

...a muddy, MAGICAL, MARVELLOUS MIRACLE!